A View from the Pew

A View from the Pew

Sketches and Monologues
About Church Life;
from the Potluck
to the Bored Meeting

A Lillenas Drama Resource

by
Martha Bolton

Lillenas Publishing Company
Kansas City, MO 64141

Dedication

To my husband, Russ,
  For always laughing at my writing
    ... even when I was trying to be serious.

Contents

Preface

Do you wake up on Sunday mornings with perfectly good intentions of getting to church on time, but never seem to make it before the benediction?

Have you ever had to sit behind a woman with a large hat and found yourself humming, "Why me, Lord?"

Have you ever been asked to substitute teach for children's church only to break out into a cold sweat and start hyperventilating right there in the foyer?

Are you suffering from potluck stress and fund-raiser burnout?

If you answered yes to any of the above, then you've picked up the right book.

"A VIEW FROM THE PEW" is a collection of sketches and monologues that deal with these subjects and more in a lighthearted and fun manner.

But, they teach us something, too.

In "The Journey Home" we learn the importance of making the pastor's sermon last longer than the trip out of the church parking lot. In "Make a Joyful Noise" we learn how working together can make beautiful music, and how not working together can make . . . well, you'll find out. And in "Excuses, Excuses, Excuses" we see there's really no excuse for staying home from church. In fact, it could prove to be one of life's most embarrassing moments.

These sketches may be performed for a variety of occasions including church banquets, dinner theaters, women's meetings, men's gatherings, illustrated sermons, Sunday School programs, or any other function where a good laugh (and look) at ourselves might be in order.

The set, costume, and prop requirements are minimal, and most of the scripts call for only two to four players.

So, if perpetual potlucks are getting you down, and board meetings tend to bore you, just remember life is so much easier when we look at it with a smile.

—MARTHA BOLTON

"Happy is that people, whose
God is the Lord."

Psalm 144:15

Acknowledgments

To Paul Miller, Ken Bible, and all my friends at Lillenas for recognizing true talent when they see it . . . but publishing me anyway.

To my sons, Rusty, Matt, and Tony, who were so excited when my first book came out that they started selling copies door-to-door to each of my neighbors (who, I might add, have all since moved).

And finally, to all the pastors and churches who encouraged me in my early writing career. (See, it's all YOUR fault!)

A View from the Pew

Get Me to the Church on Time

A Comedy Sketch

Characters:
> CARL (Father)
> AGNES (Mother)
> DAVE (Son, a teenager)
> LISA (Daughter, a preteen)
> DEACON BUSH (can be changed to any church official)

Setting:
> Four chairs signifying a car

Props:
> A car horn

▽

(Sketch opens with CARL *entering and taking the driver's seat in the car. After a few impatient moments he begins to honk the horn.)*

CARL *(honking the horn, yelling offstage):* Come on! We're going to be late for Sunday School! *(Honks horn again.)*

DAVE *(enters blow-drying his hair; saunters over and stands by the car, speaking in a very laid-back manner):* We're *always* late for Sunday School, Dad.

CARL: Yeah, well, for once I'd like to get there on time!

DAVE: But, Dad, don't you remember what happened the last time we were on time?

CARL: I know. They *claim* the pastor fainted, but I still say he just tripped over the microphone wires! ... Now, c'mon, put down that blow-dryer and let's *go!*

LISA (*enters smugly*): He *can't* just put it down, Dad! Don't you realize that blow-dryer has to be surgically removed from his hand?

DAVE: You're just jealous your hair doesn't look this great!

LISA: Now why would I want dandruff?

CARL: C'mon, both of you! It's Sunday . . . call a truce, will you?

DAVE: Just give me one more minute, Dad, and I'll be ready to go.

LISA (*sitting down in backseat of the car, opposite side of* CARL): Well, *I'm* ready now, Father. (*Looks at* DAVE) Some of us don't have to spend hours in front of a mirror.

DAVE: And I'm sure your mirror thanks you for it! (*He smiles triumphantly, then exits.*)

CARL (*to* LISA): What's keeping your mother? (*Honks horn.*)

LISA: She's still trying to decide what to wear.

CARL (*sarcastic*): Terrific! (*Looks at his watch*) If we hurry, we'll be on time for *next* Sunday's service! (*Honks horn again.*)

LISA: If it makes you feel any better, Dad, the last time I saw Mom she *did* have it narrowed down to only *six* outfits.

CARL (*sarcastic*): Great . . . I don't even *own* six outfits!

LISA: Oh, here she comes now!

(AGNES *enters and takes her seat in the front.*)

CARL (*to* AGNES): It's about time! (*to* LISA) Now go see what's keeping Dave. (LISA *exits.* CARL *turns to* AGNES.) What took you so long?

AGNES: You know when you start honking that horn I can't make a decision.

CARL: Well, we're going to be late!

AGNES: I *know* that. We're *always* late.

CARL: We *wouldn't* be late if it were up to me!

AGNES (*defensive*): Are you saying *I* make you late?

CARL (*sarcastic*): Naw! I always like to warm up the car 2½ hours before taking it out on the road.

DAVE (*enters with blow-dryer still in his hand*): I'm ready now, Dad. (*He takes his seat in the back of the car*)

CARL: You mean your hair is *finally* dry?

DAVE *(running his fingers through his hair):* Not quite . . . but I'll finish it on the way to church.

CARL: Well, all right, but now where's Lisa? *(Honks horn.)*

LISA *(enters):* I can't find Dave.

CARL *(impatient):* He's in the car! C'mon!

(LISA takes her seat in the car.)

CARL *(sighs):* I don't believe it! We're all here and ready to go . . . *finally!* *(Pretends to start engine)* Oh, no! What happened to all the gas?

AGNES: What do you mean, Dear?

CARL: I filled up the tank yesterday and now it registers empty. Where'd you go?

AGNES: Just to town and back, that's all.

CARL: What town? London?

AGNES: Don't be silly, Dear. You can't drive a car to London!

CARL: If there was a sale there, you'd try!

AGNES: Well, we have enough gas to get to church, don't we?

CARL: We'd better 'cause I'm not stopping for any. We're late enough as it is. Dave, look and see if the lane's clear.

DAVE *(turns and looks behind him):* It's clear, Dad. (CARL *makes the motion of turning the steering wheel and pulling into the flow of traffic)* Just as soon as that bus goes by.

CARL *(quick, sharp turn back to the curb; catches his breath, then s-l-o-w-l-y turns to* DAVE*):* Why did you do *that?*

DAVE: Do what, Dad?

CARL *(shaking his head):* Never mind. But I think you'd better lay off the blow-dryer for a while. It's slow-cooking your brains. Now, *(taking a deep breath)* shall we try that again?

DAVE *(turns around and looks behind him once more):* It's clear now, Dad. Trust me.

CARL: Thank you, Dave . . . *(Turns around and looks for himself)* but, I think I'd rather wait until that 18-wheeler goes by.

DAVE: He would have waited for you.

CARL: Yeah, right in my trunk! *(Waits a moment, then mimes pulling out into the flow of traffic)* There! Now let's get to Sunday School.

(Brief pause.)

AGNES: Did everyone remember to bring their Bibles?

LISA: Yeah, why?

AGNES *(pretending to glance over at speedometer):* 'Cause your father's speeding. You'd better hold them and start praying.

CARL: I'm *not* speeding. I'm just trying to get to church before all the good seats are taken.

LISA: You mean the ones in the front, Dad?

CARL: No, I mean the ones in the back. *(He starts honking at the imaginary car in front of him)* C'mon, Buddy, this isn't a parking lot! *(Honk, honk)*

AGNES: I really don't think you should be following so close to that car in front of us.

CARL: Why not? He's a *slowpoke!* *(Honk, honk)*

AGNES: Still, I don't think . . .

CARL *(cuts in):* Right! You don't think, so will you please just let me do the driving? *(Honk, honk)* Oh, this is ridiculous! I'm just going to have to pass this snail!

AGNES: All right, but when you do, wave. He's one of the deacons.

CARL: What? *(He slams on the brakes, embarrassed.)*

AGNES: That "slowpoke" you've been honking at is Deacon Bush.

CARL *(looks sick):* You're kidding. (AGNES *shakes her head*) Oh, well, it doesn't matter. He's got a "Honk if you love Jesus" bumper sticker on his car. I'll just pretend that's why I was honking.

AGNES: It just says to honk if you love Jesus. It doesn't say to play "Amazing Grace."

CARL: So, I'll tell him I got carried away. . . . Anyway, it's good to know they're going to be late, too. *(Brief pause)* Oh, no . . .

AGNES: What's the matter?

CARL: We just ran out of gas!

AGNES: Well, what are we going to do now?

CARL: We're not that far from church. Come on, Dave, get out and help me push it.

AGNES: You're going to push this car to church?

CARL (sarcastic): No! We're going to carry it! . . . Of course we're going to push it. Do you have any *other* ideas?

(CARL and DAVE *pretend to get out of the car and start pushing it.*)

LISA (sinking down in her seat): This is *so* embarrassing! I'll just never live this down! Never!

AGNES: Things could be worse, Dear.

LISA: How could they possible be worse?

AGNES: We could be on time. At least now everyone will be in their classes already.

CARL (after a few moments of huffing and puffing): All right, we're here.

AGNES: You're not going to leave it in the driveway, are you?

CARL: Well, I'm certainly *not* going to push it through the parking lot. Those speed bumps are murder.

DAVE (pointing): Let's push it over there, Dad.

CARL: Well, all right. I guess that looks easy enough. (They huff and puff some more) There! Now everyone just go straight to your class. (Looking around) Hopefully no one saw us. (AGNES and LISA exit. DAVE picks up hair dryer and starts to exit with it.) Uhh, Dave . . . Why don't you leave your blow-dryer in the car? If your hair gets any drier, Smokey the Bear will have to stand guard over it.

(DAVE puts back the blow-dryer, then exits. DEACON BUSH enters.)

DEACON BUSH (to CARL): Well, would you look who's here in time for Sunday School!

CARL (overly friendly): Deacon Bush! And how are you this fine morning?

(They both shake hands.)

DEACON BUSH: I heard you honking back on the highway.

CARL (cuts in quickly): Yeah, well . . . (laughs nervously) "Honk if you love Jesus." I got a little carried away, I guess.

19

DEACON BUSH: I thought maybe I wasn't going fast enough for you. But you know me . . . Obey the laws of the land!

CARL *(laughs nervously)*: Fast enough?! Oh, no, you were going plenty fast. I just had to get close enough so Agnes could see the bumper sticker better. She wanted to know what company printed it.

DEACON BUSH: But that's written in small print on the bottom of the sticker.

CARL: You're telling me! Why do you think I had to get so close? So, what do you say, shall we go on to class?

DEACON BUSH *(looks at watch)*: I guess we can go over there now.

CARL: Yeah *(giggles)*, better late than never, huh?

DEACON BUSH: Late? Why, you're a half hour early, Carl.

CARL: What?

DEACON BUSH: Yeah, it's standard time now. Don't tell me you forgot to set your clock back?

CARL: Uh, . . . I, uh . . . you mean, I'm on time?

DEACON BUSH: Well, don't expect us to throw you a party.

CARL: Uh, . . . no, no. It's just that I'm usually late.

DEACON BUSH: I know. Even the pastor noticed that you were on time today. . . . They're reviving him now. *(Puts his hand on CARL's shoulder)* Don't worry, he'll be all right. *(Thinks for a moment)* Say, Carl, you know if you'd start being more punctual like this, we could sure use your help in Sunday School.

CARL: Me?

DEACON BUSH: Yeah, we need someone like you. I admire a man who's not ashamed to "honk" if he loves Jesus.

CARL: Yeah, well, I do like to honk—for the Lord, you understand!

DEACON BUSH: Well, we could really use you in our Sunday School department, Carl, and the Lord would bless you for it. So, what do you say? Do you think you and your family could be on time next week?

CARL: You mean *two* Sundays in a *row*? Can the pastor's health take that?

DEACON BUSH: This time I'll give him an advanced warning. So, what do you say?

CARL *(thinks for a moment):* Yeah, why not? I kind of like getting to church on time!

DEACON BUSH *(puts his arm around* CARL'S *shoulder):* I think the Lord kind of likes it, too, Carl.

(CARL *nods in agreement. They exit.)*

The Hat

A Comedy Monologue

Character:
 GARY

Setting:
 A row of seven or eight empty chairs signifying a pew.

▽

(Sketch opens with GARY pretending to be scooting over people, trying to get to an empty seat.)

Excuse me. Excuse me. *(Grumbling to himself)* Oh, why did they have to put these pews so close together? I have to crawl over everyone's knees, and I *always* end up stepping on their toes! It's embarrassing . . . especially when they scream.

Ah, finally, an empty seat! *(Starts to sit down, then jumps up abruptly)* Oh, I'm sorry, lady. I didn't see you sitting there. *(As he continues moving down the row, he mutters to himself)* It's not *my* fault she blends in with the upholstery!

(Stopping at another chair) Excuse me, but is this seat taken? *(Brief pause)* It isn't? Good! *(Sits down, relieved. Then turns to the imaginary person sitting next to him.)* What's that? I am? Your purse, huh? *(Reaches behind him and mimes pulling out an imaginary purse from behind his back.)* Ah, yes, here it is. *(Looks it over as he hands it to her)* Uh, I hope you don't mind my saying so, but that's the strangest shaped purse I've ever seen in my life! . . . Oh, you say it didn't look like that until I sat on it? . . . Well, maybe you'll start a new trend.

(Looks straight ahead, then starts stretching his neck and moving his head in an effort to see around the person in front of him. Finally he mumbles to himself.)

Why me? Of all the places I could have picked to sit down, I had to choose a seat behind Minnie Pearl! . . . Just look at that hat! The only thing missing is the price tag! . . . No, wait a minute. There it is. *(Looks it over)* Ummm, half price. Figures! They certainly couldn't have sold anything that looks *that* ridiculous for full price!

Just look at the size of that thing! It looks like her head went condo! I bet she pays property taxes on that thing!

(Stretching to see around the hat, but to no avail) Why is it every time I come to church, I get stuck behind someone wearing a hat? All right, I admit I only come to church on Easter Sunday, but that's beside the point.

Well, one thing's for sure, I'm not going to get *anything* out of the sermon today! I mean, how can I concentrate on what the preacher has to say when I've got to stare into the *mad hatter's apartment complex* in front of me?

It's a shame, too. I understand the sermon is going to be on how we shouldn't let little things bother us. It's probably going to be a *great* sermon, but I sure won't get to enjoy it. Not *now*, anyway. After all, I can't get something out of a sermon on how not to let little things bother me when I'm stuck here in a crowded pew behind the Eiffel Tower of headgear!

I suppose I could ask her to take it off. But with my luck, she's probably bald!

I could always sit on top of a stack of hymnals, I guess . . . but I get dizzy at high altitudes.

I could move to another seat . . . but I don't think the guy on the end wants to see me again until the swelling in his toes goes down!

I'm afraid there's no escape. I'm stuck!

No! Wait a minute! I can see now! Yeah, this is great! If she'll just keep her head tilted that way, I can see perfectly. Finally, I'll be able to enjoy the sermon! Only now he's starting to talk about people who only go to church on holidays. What happened to not letting little things bother us? That's what he's supposed to be preaching on. So, why is he talking about "Easter Christians"? And why is he looking this way?

(Trying to hide behind the hat) If only the lady in front of me would tilt her head back to where it was, he couldn't see me. *(Desperately trying to dodge eye contact)* C'mon, lady, move over just a little bit. That's right. Now, just one more inch to you right. *Perfect!* He can't see me.

Now, if she'll just stay like that for the rest of the sermon, I'll have it made.

(Leans forward, and says sincerely) Psst . . . I love your hat . . . but next time, buy a bigger one! *(Continues ducking behind hat, trying to stay out of view from pastor.)*

The Potluck

A Comedy Sketch

Characters:
ALICE
BETTY

Setting:
A table with various dishes on it. It should look like an average potluck serving table. Serving spoons should be protruding from each dish.

Props:
A table
Dishes, various sizes
Serving spoons
A dish with a lid for ALICE to carry in

Costumes:
Regular dress, except BETTY should be wearing an apron over her clothes.

▽

(Sketch opens with BETTY behind the table. She is organizing the dishes, getting ready for the potluck. ALICE enters carrying her dish. She takes time to say a few words before dropping it off . . .)

ALICE: So, where do you want me to put my meat loaf?

BETTY: Down at the end with a towel over it.

ALICE: But no one will see it.

BETTY: I know. They requested it that way.

ALICE: But, this meat loaf's better than my other meat loafs!

BETTY: Well, I did notice you didn't need any help carrying it in.

ALICE: Oh, it's very tender and juicy this year!

BETTY: Deacon Bush will be happy to hear that!

ALICE: Is he still holding a grudge just because he chipped his tooth on last year's meat loaf?

BETTY: No. He's not holding any grudge. But he IS still holding his stomach!

ALICE: So, last year's meat loaf made a few people sick. No one had to go to the hospital.

BETTY: I know. You're improving!

ALICE: Well, just wait 'til you taste this one! *(She lifts the lid and shows her.)*

BETTY *(steps back, looking sick)*: What's that big lump over there? *(She points at the inside of the dish.)*

ALICE: You mean you can't tell?

BETTY: Not really.

ALICE: Why, it's a steeple, silly! I made my meat loaf to look like a church, and that's the steeple! Pretty clever, huh?

BETTY: Well, it certainly is interesting.

ALICE: So, where do you want me to put it?

BETTY: All right, set it down here. If no one takes any, we can always repave the driveway with it.

ALICE *(setting it down)*: Repave the driveway?

BETTY: Sure! What do you think we did with the leftovers of last year's meat loaf?

ALICE: Don't tell me every Sunday cars have been driving over *my* meat loaf!

BETTY: Of course not. They don't want tire damage! Most everybody just drives around it. Face it, Alice, cooking isn't one of your talents. God gave each of us certain talents, and cooking just isn't one of yours!

ALICE: But if I can't cook, then what talents *do* I have?

BETTY: Oh, I'm sure you've got something you can do.

ALICE: Like what?

BETTY: Can you sing?

ALICE: Not as well as I can cook.

BETTY: All right, that's out. . . . Can you play any type of musical instrument?

ALICE: Well, every time I cook dinner I end up playing an entire symphony on the smoke alarm.

BETTY: I'm sure you do. But I don't think there's much demand for a smoke alarmist! . . . What about art? Are you artistic at all?

ALICE (proud): I made this meat loaf church, didn't I?

BETTY: Yes, that's art I suppose. But, well, I don't think it'll stand the test of time. . . . Hey! What about acting? Can you act?

ALICE: Well, I was in a school play once. I did enjoy it a lot.

BETTY: Terrific! Listen, the drama department is holding auditions next Friday night for a play. Why don't you go try out?

ALICE: Me? In a play?

BETTY: Sure. Why not? You're a seasoned actress.

ALICE (thinks for a moment): Well, I was pretty good in the school play.

BETTY: See, you've got talent! You've just been hiding it behind an apron. . . . Look, why don't you do yourself and Julia Child a favor. Stay out of the kitchen and take to the stage! God gave you a talent. Use it! My talent is cooking. That's why I'm here. If I tried to act, I'd make people sick. But, your talent is acting. And when you try to cook . . . well, you know what I'm trying to say. We all have a place in God's kingdom.

ALICE: Friday night, huh?

BETTY: At seven o'clock.

ALICE: You really think I could do it?

BETTY: A great actress like you? Of course you can. Besides, remember the parable of the talents spoken of in Matthew 25? If you bury your talents, you'll lose them. But, if you're faithful with what God has given you, it will be multiplied back to you.

ALICE: All right, I'll go! And I'll give the best performance this church has ever seen. And we're talking standing ovations here . . . maybe even the Tony Award! . . . So, go ahead. Take my meat loaf! Repave the driveway! Repave the parking lot! Double the recipe and build a new sanctuary! You won't hurt my feelings! I know I can't cook! But

I *can* act! And no matter how big or small the part, I'll do my best. . . . I must be going now. My audience is calling me. *(Starts to walk off, then turns back)* By the way, do you think I should make some refreshments for Friday night? A little nourishment might help our acting.

BETTY: No. That's not necessary. *(Looks down at meat loaf)* As far as I know, there aren't any death scenes in the play!

The Offering

A Comedy Sketch

Characters:
  LONNIE
  LINDA

Setting:
  A church pew, elevated high enough on stage to guarantee maximum viewing.

Props:
  A purse for LINDA
  A checkbook inside the purse

▽

(Sketch opens with LONNIE *and* LINDA *sitting on a church pew. They are in the middle of an imaginary service.)*

LONNIE *(leaning over to* LINDA*)*: They're getting ready to take the offering. Give me the checkbook.

LINDA *(hesitant)*: You want the checkbook?

LONNIE: Yes. Give me the checkbook.

LINDA: You mean here . . . now?

LONNIE *(sarcastic)*: No, I mean later . . . *after* the offering! You see, that way I can walk up and give it to the preacher *during* his sermon! You know, the "personal" touch! . . . *Of course I mean now!*

LINDA: Well, all right . . . *(Hands him the checkbook)* But remember, we're in church. Save your screaming 'til we get home.

LONNIE: Now, why would I want to scream?

LINDA: You *always* scream when you look at the checkbook!

LONNIE: I don't scream. I cry.

LINDA: Well, whatever it is you do, you always make a scene!

LONNIE: Just give me the checkbook! I promise I'll remain very calm . . . no matter how many missing checks there are.

LINDA (handing him the checkbook): Now, you promised . . .

LONNIE (takes it and starts looking over the check register): Uhhh, Dear?

LINDA: Yes?

LONNIE: Where are checks 943 through 951?

LINDA: I was hoping you'd know.

LONNIE: You mean nine checks are missing?

LINDA (calmly): Nooo, Dear . . . They're not missing. Somebody has them. I just don't remember who.

LONNIE: And what about check 958?

LINDA: I think that one was to the paperboy . . .

LONNIE: Well, at least you remembered that one. (Starts to write down the figure.)

LINDA: It was either to him or the house payment.

LONNIE (stops abruptly, then takes a deep breath): Don't you think there's a bit of difference between a check to the paperboy and one for the house payment?

LINDA: Not really. They've both threatened to foreclose!

LONNIE (looking through register again): And what's this? You wrote a check to Sears for $32.98, but only deducted $12.98 from the balance?

LINDA: Oh, that. That's because I had a credit of $20.00 from my last deposit, which I purposely didn't credit into the existing balance.

LONNIE: This may sound stupid, but why would you do something like that?

LINDA: So I could buy a new dress, and it wouldn't feel like I was spending any money.

LONNIE: But how can you balance our account that way?

LINDA: Balance? Why would I want to do that? I'm not an accountant.

LONNIE (shakes head): Never mind. And what about check 973?

LINDA: It's there.

LONNIE: No it's not! You just have a row of question marks.

LINDA: I *know* that, silly! But, see . . . *(pointing)* I deducted $20.00 from our balance.

LONNIE: Oh, I see. You didn't remember who it was written to, but you did remember how much it was for.

LINDA: Not exactly.

LONNIE *(biting his lip):* How not exactly?

LINDA: Well, sometimes when I don't remember who I wrote a check to, I'll just put down $20.00. The real amount is usually more or less than $20.00. Sometimes it's more. Sometimes it's less. It all evens out.

LONNIE: But what if you write down $20.00 and it's really for $100?

LINDA: That's where my cushion comes in.

LONNIE: Cushion?

LINDA: Yeah, you know, deposits I didn't enter, checks I've voided, but didn't credit, things like that. It all adds up.

LONNIE *(shaking his head):* But, how do you expect me to write a check for the offering when I don't even know how much money we've got in the bank?!

LINDA *(patting him on the hand):* Like everyone else. By faith, Dear, by faith!

Let Them Eat Casserole

or

Why a Pastor's Worth His Weight in Gold

A Comedy Monologue

Character:
ANNOUNCER

Setting:
The pulpit (or lectern)

Props:
Pulpit (or lectern)
Microphone
Papers with announcement notes written on them

▽

(Sketch opens with ANNOUNCER *taking his place behind the pulpit or lectern.)*

I have a few announcements to make today, so I hope you'll bear with me.

The ice cream social originally scheduled for next Sunday has been changed to the last Sunday of the month. Naturally, this is so it won't conflict with the youth bake sale that was already scheduled for that Sunday. So, you'll want to make note of this.

And please remember that this is different than the after-church dollar-a-slice pie sale that will take place the first Sunday of next month. Don't forget to sign up in the foyer for that.

Our quarterly Dime-a-Dip Dinner will still be held next Sunday after the morning service as planned. Ladies, any donation will be greatly appreciated.

And also, ladies, I have been asked to announce that those of you who have not picked up your dishes from last week's after-church potluck may do so today. There were at least a dozen unmarked dishes, all with macaroni in them. So, please remember to pick up your dish after the service. Our kitchen committee says it has all the Tupperware it needs.

And men, please note our Men's Chili Cook-Off will be this Saturday night. It, of course, will be taking the place of our regular Men's Fellowship Breakfast, which normally is held on Saturday mornings.

And don't forget we are still selling tickets to our upcoming Sunday School banquet, which will be held next month.

Also, you'll want to mark your calendars for our children's church fundraising pancake breakfast, which is now just three weeks away.

And, of course, don't forget our annual All-Church Family Picnic is also coming up. As well as the progressive dinner for our young adults, and an old-fashioned country barbecue for our seniors.

And then, naturally, we want to be sure to invite everyone to join us after church tonight for our giant watermelon feast. . . . See you there!

(Starts to walk away, then suddenly turns back.)

Oh, and before I forget, do continue to encourage and uplift our pastor. Poor man. He had to take a temporary leave of absence . . . just to diet. He claims he hasn't heard his stomach growl since coming here!

But, don't worry—our hospitality committee sent over some cookies.

In Other Words

A Comedy Sketch

Characters:
NARRATOR
EUNICE
MABEL
INTERPRETER NO. 1
INTERPRETER NO. 2

Setting:
Sketch takes place in the foyer of a church

Props:
None

▽

(Sketch opens with NARRATOR *standing off to the side of the stage.)*

NARRATOR: Have you ever wondered what it would be like if an interpreter was around to explain the difference between what someone says and what's really in his heart? . . . It might sound something like this:

*(*EUNICE *and* INTERPRETER NO. 1 *enter from one side of the stage while* MABEL *and* INTERPRETER NO. 2 *enter from the other side.)*

EUNICE *(excited):* Well! Would you look who's here! Mabel Wilson! I can't tell you how much I've missed you!

INTERPRETER NO. 1: Actually, what I can't tell you is how *shocked* I am that you *finally* decided to come to church.

MABEL: Thank you, Honey. It's good to be back!

INTERPRETER NO. 2: If you missed me so much, why haven't you called?

EUNICE: You look nice.

INTERPRETER NO. 1: Nice and tan! She's probably been going to the lake every Sunday!

MABEL: Well, I *am* feeling much better.

INTERPRETER NO. 2: Didn't she know I've been sick?

EUNICE: Oh, have you been sick?

INTERPRETER NO. 1 *(sarcastic):* This ought to be good!

MABEL: Why, yes, I've been in the hospital.

INTERPRETER NO. 2: She must have known I was in the hospital. She just didn't bother to call!

EUNICE: No one ever told me you were in the hospital.

INTERPRETER NO. 1: Who's she trying to fool? They don't have sunlamps in hospitals.

MABEL: Well, I'm feeling much better now. I even did some gardening yesterday. Like my tan?

INTERPRETER NO. 2: I'd better explain this tan. She's so suspicious, she'll think I've been going to the lake every Sunday.

EUNICE: Your tan? I hadn't noticed.

INTERPRETER NO. 1: See! I *knew* she's been going to the lake every Sunday.

MABEL: So, how have you been?

INTERPRETER NO. 2 *(sarcastic):* This ought to kill an hour!

EUNICE: Oh, I've been a little under the weather.

INTERPRETER NO. 1 *(sighs):* If she only knew . . .

MABEL: You *do* look a little pale.

INTERPRETER NO. 2: Oh, what did I go and say *that* for? Now she's going to start telling me about all her operations again.

EUNICE: Well, you know I never have fully recovered from that last surgery.

INTERPRETER NO. 1: I *knew* I should have brought the pictures!

MABEL: It takes time, you know.

INTERPRETER NO. 2: I'm surprised she didn't bring the pictures.

EUNICE: Well, I think the service is about to start. You'd better go get yourself a seat.

INTERPRETER No. 1: It's been so long since she's been here, I wonder if she remembers which way to go.

MABEL: It was nice talking to you.

INTERPRETER No. 2: I'd rather have my teeth drilled.

EUNICE: It was great seeing you again, too.

INTERPRETER No. 1 (sarcastic): Believe me, it was the highlight of my day.

EUNICE: By the way, have you heard what the sermon is going to be on today?

MABEL: Yeah, it's about being two-faced.

EUNICE: Really?

MABEL: That's what I heard.

EUNICE: Boy, do I know some people who could *really* use that!

MABEL: Me, too! (sighs) Too bad they're not here!

(They walk offstage together. Both interpreters look at each other, shrug, then walk offstage behind them.)

The "Bored" Meeting

A Comedy Sketch

Characters:
>PASTOR WILLIAMS
>DEACON EDWARDS
>DEACON HUGHES
>DEACON SMITH
>DEACON STEVENS
>DEACON WOOD
>DEACON ADAMS
>MADAM SECRETARY

Setting:
A long table with seven chairs placed around it as in diagram below. The PASTOR's chair is in the center, and the remaining six chairs are for the various board members. MADAM SECRETARY's chair is off to the side.

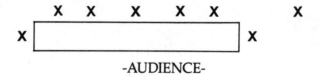

-AUDIENCE-

Costumes:
Everyone is in regular street dress except DEACON ADAMS who is in pajamas, bathrobe, and nightcap.

Props:
>Steno pad for MADAM SECRETARY
>Gavel for PASTOR WILLIAMS

▽

(Sketch opens with the PASTOR, BOARD MEMBERS, and MADAM SECRETARY in their respective places.)

PASTOR: Good evening, Brethren.

BOARD MEMBERS *(in unison)*: Good evening, Pastor Williams.

PASTOR: This meeting is now officially called to order. *(Hits gavel)* Our secretary will now call the roll. Please answer "here" if you are here, and if you are not here, kindly remain silent. *(He motions for* MADAM SECRETARY *to begin.)*

MADAM SECRETARY: Deacon Edwards?

DEACON EDWARDS: Here.

MADAM SECRETARY: Deacon Hughes?

DEACON HUGHES: Here.

MADAM SECRETARY: Deacon Smith?

DEACON SMITH: Here.

MADAM SECRETARY: Deacon Stevens?

DEACON STEVENS: Here.

MADAM SECRETARY: Deacon Wood?

DEACON WOOD: Present

PASTOR: Deacon Wood—do you *always* have to be different?

MADAM SECRETARY: And Deacon Adams?

DEACON ADAMS: I'm here, but I'd rather be home in bed!

PASTOR: Well, brethren, I do realize this was a short notice . . .

DEACON ADAMS *(straightening his bathrobe)*: You're telling me!

PASTOR: But I feel you all know me well enough to be sure I'd never call an emergency midnight board meeting unless it was for a very urgent need.

DEACON WOOD: I'd like to challenge that statement, if I may.

PASTOR: You wish to challenge that statement?

DEACON WOOD: Yes.

PASTOR: But why would you want to do that?

DEACON WOOD: So I can get my name in the minutes. I never get my name in the minutes!

PASTOR: But you have to make a motion to get your name in the minutes.

DEACON WOOD: All right, then, I so move.

PASTOR: You so move what?

DEACON WOOD: I so move that I should get my name in the minutes.

PASTOR: That's not a motion!

DEACON EDWARDS: Well, I make a motion we move on.

DEACON HUGHES: I'll second that motion.

DEACON WOOD *(to* DEACON HUGHES): Now, why would you second *his* motion, and you wouldn't second mine?

DEACON HUGHES: 'Cause your motion was stupid!

DEACON WOOD: It still needed a second!

PASTOR: Brethren . . . there's a motion on the floor. *(They all look under the table.* PASTOR *gets irritated)* You know what I mean. . . . Now, there is a motion, and it has been seconded.

DEACON WOOD *(to* DEACON HUGHES): I'll remember this!

PASTOR: Are we ready to vote on the motion?

DEACON SMITH: What was the motion?

PASTOR: Madam Secretary, could you please read back the motion?

MADAM SECRETARY: It's in shorthand.

PASTOR: So? Can't you read it?

MADAM SECRETARY: No. I can just write shorthand. I can't *read* it.

DEACON STEVENS: I remember the motion.

PASTOR: Very well, Deacon Stevens. State the motion.

DEACON STEVENS: The motion was that we move on.

DEACON SMITH: Immediately or eventually?

PASTOR *(growing more irritated):* Immediately! Now then, all in favor of moving on, please raise your hand. *(Everyone but* DEACON WOOD *raises his hand)* All opposed? (DEACON WOOD *raises his hand)* Are you dissenting?

DEACON WOOD: Will it get my name in the minutes?

PASTOR: No.

DEACON WOOD *(begrudgingly):* All right, then. *(Raises his hand again)* Make it unanimous.

PASTOR: Very well. Now, where were we? . . . Madam Secretary, could you please advise us as to where we are on our agenda?

MADAM SECRETARY: Yes, of course. You're lost!

PASTOR (sarcastic): Thank you. (Thinks for a moment) Ah, yes, now I remember. The reason I called this emergency midnight board meeting is because a very serious problem has been brought to my attention, and I feel that, as a board, we need to give it our immediate attention.

DEACON HUGHES: If it involves money, the answer is NO!

PASTOR: I'm afraid, Deacon Hughes, that money is the least of our worries.

DEACON SMITH: It sounds serious.

DEACON ADAMS: Very serious.

DEACON STEVENS: Extremely serious.

DEACON WOOD: If I agree it sounds serious, will that get my name in the minutes?

PASTOR: Deacon Wood, you are a credit to this board, and this church. But right now you're getting on my nerves! (To the board) Now . . . I do feel that before we get into a long and tiring discussion, I should advise you that regardless of the hour, we must come to a decision tonight . . . so please, bear this in mind. (DEACON STEVENS raises his hand) Yes, may we hear from Deacon Stevens?

DEACON STEVENS: Well, quite frankly, I'd like to express my views concerning this problem facing us tonight.

PASTOR: Yes? Go on.

DEACON STEVENS: I said I'd like to express my views, but I can't because you haven't told us what the problem is yet!

PASTOR: Well, I can do that now, if you like.

DEACON STEVENS: I think it would help.

PASTOR (to board): Are the rest of you brethren in agreement?

DEACON ADAMS: I consider myself ready to hear the problem.

DEACON SMITH: Me, too.

DEACON HUGHES: Yes, I think we all need to hear the problem in order to make an intelligent decision.

DEACON WOOD: You mean, this problem calls for an "intelligent" decision?

DEACON EDWARDS: *All* our problems call for an intelligent decision!

DEACON WOOD: Nobody ever told me that before.

DEACON EDWARDS: Pastor, go ahead. Tell us the problem.

PASTOR: Very well, if you're sure you're ready . . .

BOARD MEMBERS IN UNISON *(take a deep breath)*: We're ready.

PASTOR: Men . . . *(Shakes his head in anguish.)*

DEACON SMITH: Go ahead, pastor, we're behind you.

PASTOR: Men . . . next month we have scheduled the third Saturday to be the date of our annual church picnic.

DEACON ADAMS: The third Saturday?

PASTOR: Yes, this is what we had decided upon at our last emergency meeting.

DEACON ADAMS: May I see the minutes? (MADAM SECRETARY *hands him the minutes. He looks them over)* Yes, you're right . . . but I still fail to see what the problem is.

PASTOR: The problem is this, gentlemen . . . *(He buries his head in his hand for a moment)* Brethren . . . *(he looks up solemnly)* should we have the picnic potluck, or should each family member merely bring enough food for their immediate family?

DEACON EDWARDS: Oh, no! I had hoped it wouldn't come to this!

PASTOR: Deacon Edwards, I am sure we all share in that feeling, but it *has* come to this, and we cannot avoid it any longer. The decision must be made, and it must be made *tonight*.

DEACON SMITH: Well, we've always had it potluck in the past . . . as long as I can remember being on the board.

PASTOR: Yes, but has it proved to be the best method?

DEACON STEVENS: Well, I agree with Deacon Smith. Potluck has always been acceptable in the past.

PASTOR: But let's consider this. Should we leave here tonight having decided upon potluck, that is, providing all were in agreement according to parliamentary laws, what assures us that we will not end up with 20 salads and only two main dishes?

DEACON SMITH: He has a point.

DEACON EDWARDS: Then would potluck be acceptable if we had some assurance that this type of imbalance would not occur?

PASTOR: Yes, but how could we . . .

DEACON EDWARDS (cuts in): I would move we instigate some form of sign-up list to be placed in the back of the church for the congregation to sign to indicate what type of dish they will be bringing.

DEACON HUGHES: And just how much will this paper cost us?

DEACON ADAMS: I'll donate the paper!

DEACON HUGHES: You'll donate the paper?

DEACON ADAMS: I'll donate anything just so I can get home and go to bed!

PASTOR: Very well, we do have a motion on the floor . . . (All board members look under the table again) Will you quit that! We do have a motion, does it have a second?

DEACON HUGHES: I'll second it.

DEACON WOOD: Sure! You always second his motions!

PASTOR: We have a motion, and it has been seconded. Are we ready to vote?

DEACON STEVENS: Was the motion to list the dishes by category alone or by individual recipes, so to speak?

PASTOR: Deacon Edwards, would you please clarify your motion?

DEACON EDWARDS: I didn't actually specify how they would list it, but I can make an amendment to the motion. The amendment would state that the dishes be listed by category alone.

PASTOR: Very well, is there a second to the amendment?

DEACON HUGHES: I'll second the amendment.

DEACON WOOD: Naturally.

PASTOR: All right, all those in favor say, "Aye." (Everyone but DEACON WOOD says aye.) All those opposed say, "Nay."

DEACON WOOD: Nay.

PASTOR (to DEACON WOOD): I'm sorry, but that won't get your name in the minutes either.

DEACON WOOD: That's all right. I've got to vote my convictions.

PASTOR: Very well, motion has been carried. Now then, we will need someone to be responsible for posting the list in the back of the church.

DEACON EDWARDS: I would move that Deacon Hughes be in charge of that.

DEACON HUGHES: I'm sorry, but I'm going to have to decline this honor. However, I would like to make the motion that Deacon Smith become the chairman for this in my stead.

DEACON SMITH: I am, indeed, honored; however, I am also forced to decline, but I'd like to nominate Deacon Stevens. I know he'd do a fine job!

DEACON STEVENS: I would rather see Deacon Adams take the position.

DEACON ADAMS: This is going to be a busy month for me. How about you, Pastor Williams?

DEACON EDWARDS: Yes, I'll second that.

PASTOR: Very well. All in favor say, "Aye." *(It's unanimous)* All opposed? *(silence)* Very well, then, it has been moved and carried. Deacon Wood will be in charge of posting the list.

DEACON WOOD: But, pastor, *you* were elected. Why did you appoint me?

PASTOR: I just wanted to make sure you got your name in the minutes! Meeting adjourned! *(Hits gavel.)*

The Substitute Children's Church Worker

A Comedy Monologue

Character:
   SUE HARDING—long-suffering, but a little overwhelmed with children

Setting:
   She is standing in front of an imaginary children's church class.

Props:
   A long roll of paper with scribbles on it, such as an adding machine tape

▽

(*Sue smiles at the children*) Good morning, class. My name is Sue Harding, and I'll be your substitute teacher for children's church today. Your regular teacher will be back next week. She just needed a little rest. It seems she was starting to talk to the hymnals.

(*She begins to slowly walk back and forth in front of the class as she talks*) Now, before we begin I probably should confess I'm not used to working with children. It's never really been . . . well, how should I put it—"my calling"—still, I promised your teacher I'd take over for her today, so here I am. (*Mumbling under her breath in a prayer*) God, help me!

But please don't feel guilty because you're making me miss out on the sermon, or because I'm probably forfeiting a tremendous blessing just to sit in here with you children. After all, it's not *your* fault I couldn't think of an excuse fast enough when your teacher called me!

Next time, though, she won't catch me off guard. You see, I've written down a few all-purpose excuses (*Takes roll of paper out of pocket, i.e., the adding machine tape with scribbles on it. Holding one end of the roll of paper she lets it roll*) And I'll be ready for her!

Now, then, I see you're all wearing name tags. That should help me a lot. *(Pretends to be reading one of the children's name tags.)* Uh . . . Johnny? Is that your name? *(Brief pause)* Well, first of all, Johnny, I wonder if you would be so kind as to get down off the table? Thank you, and bring that chair down with you! . . . Yes, I know the janitor put it up there, but I don't think he really meant for you to sit on it up there.

Now, what I thought we'd do today is—*(Looks around, sees Mary's hand is raised)* Yes, Mary? You say Matthew is pulling your ponytail? *(To Matthew)* Matthew, why are you pulling Mary's ponytail? *(Pause)* You're just seeing if it's real? . . . Well, do her excruciating screams convince you? . . . Good! Now, then, why don't you move over there by Brian? . . . What's that, Matthew? . . . You say Brian always hits you? . . . But, Brian is wearing a suit. *Everyone* knows that little boys in suits don't hit! Now, go on . . . Trust me. *(Smiles encouragingly)* That's right . . . go on. *(She turns back to the rest of the class, smiles, then quickly turns back toward Brian and Matthew)* Brian! What'd you do *that* for? . . . Well, I'm sorry, but that's NOT how you say hello!

Matthew, you can go sit over there by Carla.

Now, then . . . where were we? *(Pointing)* Yes, Heidi? . . . Johnny's on the table again? *(Turns and looks)* No, no, Johnny, you *must* stay down from there! . . . Look, you've got the other children trying stunts now . . . and that chandelier won't hold everybody!

And George, please don't invert your eyelids like that! Not only does it look awful, but you'll go blind! Trust me. I know these things!

And Joey, I don't think clip-on ties were made for your nose. Kindly put yours back on your shirt! *(Pause)* What do you mean, it's stuck? . . . Well, just *unclip* it! I mean, you certainly can't go through life with a red tie clipped to your nose! You'd look silly, and it'll limit your wardrobe!

(Suddenly holds ears and screams) Kevin! *(She closes her eyes, takes a deep breath, then says slowly)* Don't you ever run your fingernails down a chalkboard again! There are laws against that, you know!

Peter, why are you stacking the chairs on top of each other like that? . . . No, it's *not* time to go! We still have 20 minutes left! *(Looks at her watch)* Well, actually, we have 19 minutes left, but who's counting?

Joey, haven't you got that tie off yet? *(Brief pause)* Well, come here, I'll help you. *(She pretends to unclip it from his nose and attach it to his shirt)* There! Now, doesn't it look better on your neck? . . . Please, go back to your seat . . . and next time dress casual.

(Looks toward rear of classroom) Rusty! Get away from the refreshments! *(Brief pause)* What do you mean you didn't touch them? I can see the Oreo bulges in your cheeks from here! . . . Well, go ahead and finish the 10 you've already got in your mouth, then take your seat.

(To class) Hey! I know what! *(She claps her hands together in excitement)* How about if I tell you kids a story? Would you like that? *(Pause)* You would? OK, then everyone come sit down in a circle. . . . A circle,

Tony, not a pile! . . . That's it, c'mon. Now, let's see. I know you've all heard the story of how much Jesus loves you, so I won't . . . What's that, Michael? *(Brief pause)* You've *never* heard about how He came to earth and was born in a manger . . . then later gave His life on the Cross for you and me. . . . No one ever told you about Him?

I see you're wearing a visitor's tag. Is this your family's first Sunday here? *(Brief pause)* Oh, you did? You came alone? You mean, you *walked* here by yourself? *(Mumbles to herself)* And to think I almost didn't come because the air-conditioning in my car wasn't working!

Well, I'll tell you what, why don't you sit over here by me, Michael, and I'll tell you and the class all about this Man called Jesus! *(Smiles)* He loves you very, very much, you know. He said, "Suffer the little children to come unto Me, for of such is the kingdom of God." You see, to Jesus there's nothing quite as precious as childlike faith . . . and you kids have a corner on the market!

Why, Michael, you got up and walked to church this morning . . . ALL BY YOURSELF! You didn't know anyone here. You just knew you wanted to go to church. No wonder Jesus loves the little children! Do you realize how many adults are still in bed at this very moment just thinking of excuses why they can't go to church? The car's too dirty, the lawn needs mowing, the fence needs mending, nothing to wear! Excuses! . . . Sometimes I think we adults have the corner on that market!

(Thoughtfully) And speaking of excuses . . . *(Walks over and picks up the roll of excuses from off the floor. Looks it over thoughtfully.)* I guess I've been collecting a few myself!

You know, Michael, you may not understand this, but I think YOU were the teacher today.

Make a Joyful Noise

A Comedy Sketch

Characters:
> HOWARD
> MIKE
> Five or six choir members

Setting:
> A mock choir loft or something the choir members may stand on to be at different levels

Props:
> Choir books or hymnals for each character

Costumes:
> Choir robes, if available

▽

(Sketch opens with HOWARD, MIKE, *and the rest of the* CHOIR MEMBERS *standing in their places. They are just finishing a song.)*

EVERYONE *(singing):* Ahhhhhhh . . . mennnnnnn.

(At the conclusion of "Amen" they turn the page in their choir books to prepare for the next number.)

HOWARD *(turning to* MIKE *who is standing next to him):* Do you have to sing so loud?

MIKE: If I want to be heard over *you,* yes, I do!

HOWARD: Well, *I'm* supposed to be loud. After all, I *am* the number one soloist in the church!

MIKE: That may be, but unless your name is "Unison," we were *all* supposed to be singing *together.*

HOWARD: All right! But the least you could do is sing the right notes!

MIKE: I *was* singing the right notes!

HOWARD: Well, they may have been the right notes, but they went to a different song.

MIKE: Are you saying I can't sing?

HOWARD: I'm saying when David wrote, "Make a joyful *noise* unto the Lord," he was directly referring to you!

MIKE: Well, the choir director must think my voice is just as good as yours.

HOWARD: Whatever makes you think that?

MIKE: He put us next to each other, didn't he?

HOWARD: Yes, but that's only so I can drown you out!

MIKE: I'll have you know whenever *I* sing a solo, there isn't a dry eye in the audience.

HOWARD: When *you* sing a solo, there aren't *any* eyes in the audience! Everyone gets up and leaves!

MIKE: And I suppose you sing like a bird?

HOWARD: I've been known to receive standing ovations.

MIKE: Only when you sing during the benediction!

HOWARD: Well, listen. I have the next solo, so why don't you do the audience a big favor?

MIKE: What's that? Dismiss them?

HOWARD (*laughs sarcastically*): You know when we come to that part where the choir is supposed to join in?

MIKE: You mean the chorus?

HOWARD: Yes, the chorus. You know where I sing the first part of each line, and they sing the rest of it?

MIKE: Yes?

HOWARD: Well, why don't you do us all a favor and just lip-synch it?

MIKE: You mean, you don't want me to sing?

HOWARD: Hey, don't take it personal. Actually, I'd rather no one sang with me.

MIKE: But, don't you realize it takes more than one person to make a choir?

HOWARD: Whoever said that obviously had never heard *me* sing!

MIKE: Even if you've got a beautiful voice, being in the choir takes *team-work!*

HOWARD: Well, *I'm* up to bat now, so just keep it quiet in the bleachers!

MIKE: All right, if that's the way you want it.

HOWARD: That's the way I want it. You just lip-synch, OK? The rest of the choir can do whatever they want to. I really don't need them either.

MIKE: You mean you don't need any of us?

HOWARD: Actually, no. But, they're supposed to sing the last part of each line in the chorus.

MIKE: But, you'd rather sing all by yourself?

HOWARD: Of course, I'd rather sing all by myself! But, it's too late now. Excuse me—my spotlight is waiting.

(HOWARD *struts over to the side of the stage, smiles at the audience, turns and smiles at the choir, then looks back at the audience. As soon as his head is turned back to the audience, the rest of the choir members look at* MIKE, *who in turn looks at them. They all nod in agreement.* HOWARD *then nods to the accompanist who begins introduction to "Working Together" (see below).* HOWARD *sings verse one as a solo, then joins with the chorus, which is only the first two words on each line. After singing his part, he turns to the* CHOIR, *but they don't sing their part. Instead, they just smile while the accompanist plays their part. Throughout the chorus* HOWARD *keeps trying to give the* CHOIR *the eye to start singing their part, but they just smile. The* CHOIR *is obviously teaching* HOWARD *a lesson about teamwork. At the end of the two verses, and two very embarrassing choruses,* HOWARD *sings the final line: "Working together—forevermore." He then turns and makes his way back to the choir loft.*)

Working Together

MARTHA BOLTON

(Solo)

LYNDELL LEATHERMAN

1. Work-ing to - geth - er seems__ so right;
2. No__ one the bet - ter, all __ the same.

MIKE *(smiling):* I do believe that was the *best* solo you've ever sung!

HOWARD *(gritting his teeth so the audience doesn't see that he's mad):* Why did you do that?

MIKE: Yes, sir, not a dry eye in the audience! They were all laughing too hard!

HOWARD: *Why did you do that?*

MIKE: Well, you said you'd rather sing it alone! You said you didn't need any of us!

HOWARD *(swallowing his pride):* All right! I admit it! I need you guys!

MIKE: Do you mean it?

HOWARD: Yes, I mean it.

MIKE: *Really* mean it?

HOWARD: Yes, I *really* mean it!

MIKE: Even me?

HOWARD: Yes, even you.

MIKE: Say it!

HOWARD: I need *even* you!

MIKE *(smiles):* Good! *Now* we can sing!

EVERYONE *(singing in unison):* Working together—forevermore!

Super-Pastor

A Comedy Sketch

Characters:
> NARRATOR
> SUPER-PASTOR
> WOMAN
> MAN

Setting:
> No special set required.

Props:
> Woman's purse (large enough to hold her particular props)
> Man's briefcase (large enough to hold his particular props)
> Doughnut (glazed doughnut suggested only because it's the author's favorite)
> Fake beard
> Nonoffensively trendy item, i.e., jewelry, glittery vest, bandana, etc.
> Glasses (preferably black rimmed)
> Kiddie hat
> Handcuffs
> Blindfold
> Wad of fake money

Special Costume:

Super-Pastor T-shirt (any T-shirt with the word "Super-Pastor" written on it). This is to be worn under a regular business suit. Also, Super-Pastor should be wearing a nice-looking wig over a skinhead cap. He also needs a cape.

▽

(Sketch opens with SUPER-PASTOR *standing center stage with his hands on his hips, holding his chest out. He has that, well, how shall we say it . . . "heroic" look.* NARRATOR *is standing to the side of the stage.)*

NARRATOR: *Quicker than a sermonette.*
> *More mighty than a nine-point message.*
> *Capable of living from Sunday to Sunday on a single compliment . . .*

Who is this amazing, incredible stupendous, wonderfully courageous person, you ask? *Why, it's Super-Pastor . . .* of course!

(SUPER-PASTOR *rips off his shirt and coat to reveal T-shirt with the word super-pastor written on it. Also attached is the official super-pastor cape.*)
Super-Pastor, a dedicated servant of the one true God, fighting an endless battle for love, appreciation, . . . and . . . just a little understanding!

(MAN *with briefcase holding his props, and* WOMAN *with large purse holding her props, approach* SUPER-PASTOR *and look him over, curiously. As they circle him, they begin critiquing our hero. Naturally, with each compliment, he smiles, and with each criticism, he frowns. Needless to say, his facial muscles end up getting quite a bit of exercise. Also, with each criticism, his shoulders begin to droop, and his head begins to hang down.*)

WOMAN: Super-Pastor, huh? *(Examines cape)* Nice cape, but his sermons are too long. Doesn't he know people want to get home so they can eat?

MAN: His messages are good, but they're way too short! What's he trying to do . . . get home quick so he can eat?

WOMAN: He's too strict!

MAN: He's too weak!

WOMAN *(covering her ears)*: He's much too loud!

MAN *(cupping his hand over his ear)*: I wish he'd speak up!

WOMAN: And he's way too tall! *(She squashes him down, trying to make him look shorter.)*

MAN: No, no! He's too short! Much too short! *(He stretches him to look taller again.)*

WOMAN: He's definitely too skinny! *(She takes the doughnut from her purse and shoves it in his mouth.)*

MAN: Are you kidding? Look at those cheeks! *(Yanks doughnut from his mouth.)* Gluttony is a sin, you know.

WOMAN: He's too young and spunky. He needs more maturity. *(Puts fake beard on him)* There, that makes him look older!

MAN: Well, I say he's too old-fashioned! He needs to get "with it." *(Puts nonoffensive "trendy" item on him, i.e., bandana, jewelry, or whatever is the trend. The key word here, however, is "nonoffensive.")*

WOMAN: I don't like how he parts his hair. *(She pulls off his wig, revealing skinhead underneath.)*

MAN (rubbing skinhead): What hair? He doesn't have any!

WOMAN: I say he needs to look more intelligent! (She puts a pair of glasses on him) There, that's much better!

MAN: No, no, no. He needs to talk down more. He's overeducated as it is. (Puts kiddie hat on him.)

WOMAN: Well, I have to admit he's grossly underpaid! (She tucks a wad of bills under his collar.)

MAN: Hey! I'm grossly underpaid! (Grabs the money and pockets it himself) God will take care of him!

WOMAN: My biggest complaint is he's never around when you need him! (She cuffs herself together with him.)

MAN: Well, personally, I just wish he'd stay out of my life. He's too concerned! I say what he doesn't know won't hurt him! (He blindfolds him.)

WOMAN (looks him over): You know, for a "Super-Pastor," he sure turned out to be . . .

MAN: Human?

WOMAN: Yeah, that's the word I'm looking for. Human! (She uncuffs herself and starts to walk off.)

MAN (looks him over): It's a shame, too. He had such great possibilities!

(They exit.)

NARRATOR: Super-Pastor . . . if he tried to please everyone, he'd probably look like this . . . (he looks toward SUPER-PASTOR) And so . . . (SUPER-PASTOR begins taking off the props) . . . our "hero" continues to fight an endless battle . . . (the props should be off now, and SUPER-PASTOR stands, proudly, with his hands on his hips once again) . . . for love, appreciation . . . and just a little understanding!
So, folks, the next time you see your "super" pastor, why don't you tell him you love him just the way he is! Go ahead! Make his day!

The Journey Home

A Comedy Sketch

Characters:
EDGAR
MARTHA

Setting:
Two chairs signifying a car

▽

(Scene opens with EDGAR *and* MARTHA *sitting in their car. Church has just let out, and they are heading home.)*

EDGAR: That was sure a good sermon, wasn't it, Martha?

MARTHA: Yes, Dear, it certainly was.

EDGAR: "He that is slow to anger is better than the mighty . . ." Proverbs 16:32. I'm going to try to remember that.

MARTHA: Me, too. *(Brief pause)* Uhh, Sweetheart . . . don't you think you're following just a little too close to that car in front of us?

EDGAR: Too close? He's at least 40 feet in front . . . *(Stops abruptly remembering the sermon. Then says calmly . . .)* Maybe you're right, Dear. I'll try to watch that.

MARTHA *(smiles):* Remember the sermon, Honeyface. "He that is slow to anger is better than the mighty."

EDGAR: Yeah, what a scripture, huh?

MARTHA: You just went through a red light.

EDGAR: It wasn't red. It was yellow.

MARTHA: It was both. It was yellow, then it turned red just as you entered the intersection.

EDGAR: I'm sorry, but it was yellow! It turned red AFTER I was already *in* the intersection!

MARTHA: Well, it certainly wasn't *green!* So, why don't you slow down and try to find some *green* ones for a change?

EDGAR *(biting his lip, he begins to quote the scripture):* "He that is slow to anger is better than the mighty. He that is slow to anger is better than the mighty. He that is . . ."

MARTHA *(cuts in):* What are you doing?

EDGAR: Just some memory work, Dear. That's such a good scripture, I want to always remember it. *(Under his breath)* Especially when I'm in the car with you!

MARTHA: What was that?

EDGAR: I said I think I'm coming down with the flu.

MARTHA: Well, the sooner you pass that car in front of us, the sooner we'll get home! He's a slowpoke!

EDGAR: Pass him? But I thought you wanted me to slow down!

MARTHA: Slow down, yes . . . but you don't have to park! C'mon, pass him!

EDGAR: All right, but I'm going to have to speed up to do it!

MARTHA: I *know* that!

EDGAR *(turns imaginary wheel to mime passing the slower car, then mimes pulling back into the original lane):* There! Are you happy now?

MARTHA: I will be as soon as you slow down!

EDGAR: But you told me to speed up to pass that car!

MARTHA: And have you passed him?

EDGAR: Yes!

MARTHA: So, now you can slow down!

EDGAR: You mean I passed him just so I could slow down in front of him?

MARTHA: Isn't that what *everybody* does?

EDGAR: But . . .

MARTHA *(cutting in):* Anyway, you should probably be getting over. We're going to be turning soon, you know.

EDGAR: There's still plenty of time.

MARTHA *(turns and looks behind her):* But, it's clear now, Puddinglump.

EDGAR: But I don't want to change lanes now, *(biting his lip)* Bunnybreath.

MARTHA *(ignoring his protest):* Go ahead . . . start signaling.

EDGAR: I said I don't want to change lanes yet.

MARTHA: Why not?

EDGAR: For two reasons.

MARTHA: Yes?

EDGAR: Number one . . . I'm the boss.

MARTHA: Next?

EDGAR: And number two . . . I don't want to! Not yet, anyway!

MARTHA: But it's clear now!

EDGAR: Well, I'm *not* changing lanes now!

MARTHA: Don't you raise your voice at me!

EDGAR: *I'm not raising my voice!*

MARTHA: Boy! What happened to the ol' "He that is slow to anger is better than the mighty"?

EDGAR: Yeah, well, it's obvious that the writer of that scripture had never driven in a car with you!

MARTHA: And what's *that* supposed to mean?

EDGAR: It means if he had, he would have written a disclaimer!

MARTHA: Oh, he would would he?

EDGAR: Maybe even an extra chapter . . . just to cover this situation!

MARTHA: That does it! I'm not going to speak to you for a month!

EDGAR: Good! That's the *only* time we ever communicate!

MARTHA: But just one thing before I start ignoring you . . .

EDGAR: What's that?

MARTHA: I want to know if you're ready to change lanes now or not?

EDGAR: I said I'll do it when I'm good and ready!

MARTHA: Well, you just passed our street!

EDGAR *(turns and looks over his shoulder)*: I did?

MARTHA *(leans back in her seat, satisfied)*: Now, my silence begins!

EDGAR: Big deal! So, I passed our street, I'll just go around the block.

MARTHA: Fine . . . you do that!

EDGAR: Oh, I thought you weren't talking!

MARTHA: That's the last word you'll hear from me!

EDGAR: Good!

MARTHA: . . . And another thing . . . I hope you DO go around the block!

EDGAR: Why? So you can say "I told you so" all the way?

MARTHA: Nothing would make me happier!

EDGAR: Well, in that case I think I'll just make a U-turn right here!

MARTHA: You can't make a U-turn here!

EDGAR: Oh, no? *Watch me! (He makes motion of turning wheel.)*

MARTHA: Happy now? . . . I watched you. The people on the corner watched you. And that policeman over there watched you!

EDGAR: *What* policeman?

MARTHA: The one putting his red lights and siren on.

EDGAR *(looks in rearview mirror)*: Oh, him.

MARTHA: Well, aren't you going to pull over?

EDGAR: I was waiting for *you* to tell me to. After all, doesn't he know you're the *final* authority?

MARTHA: Just pull over before he drags out the bullhorn!

EDGAR: Even if he did, I *still* couldn't hear him over *your* mouth!

MARTHA: Are you saying I've got a big mouth!

EDGAR: I'm saying you could swallow Idaho!

MARTHA: Make that *two* months that I'm not going to speak to you!

EDGAR: Face it, Martha, you're a backseat driver! You've *always* been a backseat driver! Your mother even says you used to give her directions from your stroller!

MARTHA: Only when she'd get lost. Anyway, you can say what you want, but I'm not the one getting a ticket!

EDGAR (*pretends to pull over; then turning his head to his left, he talks to imaginary officer*): Yes, officer, is something wrong? (*Brief pause*) An illegal U-turn? I don't know . . . but wait, just a minute. This is my wife. I'll ask her. (*Turns toward Martha*) Martha, Honey, Sweetheart, Dear . . . did you see me make an illegal U-turn back there?

MARTHA (*leaning forward to talk to the officer*): I *told* him not to do it, officer!

EDGAR (*looking somewhat ill*): I'm sorry officer, I must have made a mistake. . . . No, not about the U-turn. About the introduction. (*Looking over at Martha*) This is my *ex*-wife! (*Gives her a sour look, then turns back toward the officer*) All right, where should I sign? (*Mimes signing the ticket*) Thank you, officer. And believe me, it won't happen again! (*Looks at Martha*) Well, shall we go home now, or would you rather I serve time?

MARTHA: Are you mad at me, Honey?

EDGAR: Me? Mad at you? *Are you kidding?* (*Starts quoting the scripture to himself*) "He that is slow to anger is better than the mighty. He that is slow to anger is better than the mighty. He that is . . ."

MARTHA (*cuts in*): I guess I've been making it difficult for you, huh, Sweetcheeks?

EDGAR: Well, they *do* say temptation worketh patience. Anyway, I suppose the ticket was my own fault.

MARTHA: Yeah, but you probably wouldn't have missed our street in the first place if I hadn't been nagging you.

EDGAR: Look, what do you say we just go home and forget any of this ever happened.

MARTHA: Oh, Honey, I'd love that!

EDGAR: We won't say another word about this! I deserved the ticket, so I'll just pay it, and we'll forget this whole entire episode!

MARTHA: Sounds good to me, Loveblossom.

EDGAR: We'll totally erase the last 15 minutes from our minds!

MARTHA: That's right! We'll pretend this is the church parking lot, and we're starting over!

EDGAR: All right, let's see . . . church just let out, and we got in our car, and I said, "That was sure a good sermon, wasn't it, Martha?"

MARTHA: And I said, "Yes, Dear, it certainly was."

EDGAR: Then I said, " 'He that is slow to anger is better than the mighty . . . ' " Proverbs 16:32.

MARTHA: And then you said you were going to try to remember that!

EDGAR: And you said you were, too. So, now, we'll take it from there . . . like nothing else ever happened!

MARTHA: Right!

EDGAR: I'll just pull out into the traffic and head home . . .

MARTHA: Right! *(Turns and looks behind her)* . . . Just as soon as I tell you it's clear!

Blackout

Patience, Brother

A Comedy Sketch

Characters:
>HUBERT
>GEORGINE
>WAITRESS

Setting:
>A table with two chairs

Props:
>Two menus
>Two plates of food
>Two coffee cups
>Place settings
>Coffeepot with coffee

Costumes:
>Regular dress for HUBERT and GEORGINE
>A waitress outfit or an apron for the waitress

▽

(Sketch opens with HUBERT and GEORGINE entering from side of stage. They pause to speak to imaginary hostess.)

HUBERT *(to imaginary hostess):* Table for two, please. *(Brief pause)* You're kidding? A 20 minute wait? *(To wife)* If the preacher had quit preaching after his first "In closing," we could have beat the rush!

GEORGINE: It may not take that long. *(Looks toward table)* See, there's some people leaving now.

HUBERT: Good! I hate waiting!

GEORGINE: Didn't you get anything out of the sermon this morning? It was on patience, you know.

HUBERT: Of course, it was on patience! It took the patience of Job to sit through all those "In closings"!

GEORGINE: He only said three "In closings."

HUBERT: Three "In closings," two "In summations," and one "In conclusion"!

GEORGINE: You counted?

HUBERT: It's my ministry!

GEORGINE: Well, even so, he only ran over a few minutes.

HUBERT: A few minutes seems like an eternity when your stomach's growling!

GEORGINE: Was that *your* stomach growling? I was wondering why the choir kept staring at us!

HUBERT *(looks over toward table)*: Look! I think that table over there is clear now. *(Grabbing her arm)* C'mon, let's go!

GEORGINE *(hesitant)*: But the hostess didn't call our name. She called the Jenkins party.

HUBERT: Do you *really* think she's going to check our I.D.? C'mon, let's grab it before the Jenkins party has time to get up! *(He yanks her, and they rush over to table and sit down.)*

GEORGINE *(panting)*: You really should learn to be more patient. All good things come to those who wait, you know!

HUBERT: Yeah? Well, tell that to the Jenkins party!

(WAITRESS enters with coffeepot and menus. She hands them their menus.)

WAITRESS: Coffee?

(They both nod. She pours their coffee, which looks more like ink, then exits.)

GEORGINE *(looking at coffee, unimpressed)*: Interesting blend.

HUBERT: Cream and sugar?

GEORGINE: No, just a knife to stir it with!

HUBERT *(looking over menu)*: So, have you decided what you want?

GEORGINE *(looking over menu, hesitantly)*: Yeah, a new menu!

HUBERT: Well, just be ready to order when the waitress comes back. The last waitress I had here retired after handing me the menu.

GEORGINE: So, then why did you insist on coming here today?

HUBERT: They take coupons.

GEORGINE (*rolls her eyes*): The last of the big spenders!

HUBERT: Hey! I let loose with a bundle today, or didn't you see me drop that 20 dollar bill into the offering plate this morning?

GEORGINE: Yeah, I saw you. But you took back 15 dollars in change!

HUBERT: What's wrong with that?

GEORGINE: You made a scene!

HUBERT: Well, it wasn't *my* fault he only had ones! (*Looks up*) Here comes the waitress. Do you know what you're going to have?

GEORGINE: After eating here . . . probably heartburn!

HUBERT: The food's good here. Trust me. After all, doctors even eat here.

GEORGINE: How do you know that?

HUBERT: There's an ambulance parked out back.

GEORGINE: Probably just another satisfied customer!

(WAITRESS *enters and walks over to table.*)

WAITRESS (*chewing gum*): So, what'll it be?

HUBERT: Uhh, I think I'll have the hot roast beef sandwich.

WAITRESS: And you, Missy?

GEORGINE: I'll have the same, I guess. (*Under her breath*) It'll make it easier on the coroner!

WAITRESS (*writes down the order*): Would you folks care for an appetizer today?

GEORGINE (*looks around with just a hint of nausea*): No, I think it's too late for that!

(WAITRESS *takes menus, and exits just long enough to grab the two plates of roast beef.*)

HUBERT (*to* GEORGINE): So, now, what do you . . . (*looks up and sees waitress entering with plates*) Wow! That was fast! (WAITRESS *sets down the plates and exits*) They probably make up a bunch of these plates ahead of time.

GEORGINE (*suspicious*): Yeah, like around Christmas!

HUBERT: Well, that's fine with me! I hate waiting! (*Starts eating.*)

GEORGINE: Hebrews 10:36, Dear. "Ye have need of patience."

HUBERT (*still eating*): Why do I have to be patient now? The food's here!

GEORGINE: You haven't said the blessing.

HUBERT: You don't expect me to pray here in front of all these people, do you?

GEORGINE: If they ordered the roast beef, they'd probably appreciate it!

HUBERT: Oh, all right. (*Bows head. Then* GEORGINE *bows her head*) Dear Lord, bless this food. Amen.

GEORGINE (*looks up*): This food's going to take more than that!

HUBERT (*resumes eating*): Well, the Lord knows I'm in a hurry.

GEORGINE: You're *always* in a hurry!

HUBERT: Of course, I am! Being patient never got anyone anywhere! If you want something in life, you've got to go for it! You can't sit back and wait for it to come to you! You've got to reach out and grab it! Nice guys and patient guys always finish last! (*Suddenly, there's some excited yelling offstage.* HUBERT *turns around*) What in the world?

GEORGINE (*puzzled*): I wonder what's going on.

(WAITRESS *enters with coffeepot.*)

HUBERT: Excuse me, miss. But what's all the commotion over there about?

WAITRESS: Oh, someone just won a trip to Hawaii for being our 10 thousandth customer.

HUBERT (*excited*): You're kidding! Who was it?

WAITRESS: Some guy named "Jenkins." (GEORGINE *looks at* HUBERT. HUBERT *looks sick.* WAITRESS *pours coffee, then smiles*) Enjoy your dinner. (WAITRESS *exits.*)

The Perfect Church

A Comedy Sketch

Characters:
> Lou Ann
> Grace
> Manicurist No. 1
> Manicurist No. 2

Setting:

A beauty parlor. Needed are four chairs and two small manicurist tables. The chairs should be arranged as pictured:

The two end chairs are facing inward, and the two center chairs are back to back. The small manicurist tables are between each set of chairs.

Props:

Two manicure sets

Costumes:

Manicurists should be wearing smocks.

▽

(Sketch opens with Lou Ann *sitting in chair B.* Manicurist No. 1 *is sitting in chair A, and is giving her a manicure.)*

MANICURIST No. 1: So, tell me, Lou Ann, how did that program at your church turn out?

Lou Ann: It was very good, I must admit. *(Brief pause)* But, I've been doing some serious thinking lately.

MANICURIST No. 1: About what?

Lou Ann: Oh, about changing churches.

MANICURIST No. 1: Really?

Lou Ann: Yeah.

MANICURIST NO. 1: Why? I thought you liked your church.

LOU ANN: I do. But, well, it just doesn't seem to have everything I want in a church.

(MANICURIST NO. 2 *enters with* GRACE. LOU ANN'S *back is to them, so she doesn't see them enter.* GRACE *sits down in chair C, and* MANICURIST NO. 2 *sits in chair D. They begin the manicure.*)

MANICURIST NO. 1 (*resuming her conversation with* LOU ANN): But, I still don't understand why you'd want to change churches. I thought you said your church had the best choir you'd ever heard.

LOU ANN: Well, yes, that's true. We do have a fabulous choir. But, we're lacking so much in our Sunday School department.

GRACE (*to* MANICURIST NO. 2): Listen to that lady behind me. What I wouldn't give for a good choir! All *my* church thinks about is the Sunday School department. We've got the best Sunday School in the state, but our choir leaves a lot to be desired.

LOU ANN (*to* MANICURIST NO. 1): And it's not just our Sunday School department that's lacking, it's our women's ministries, too.

MANICURIST NO. 1: You don't have any women's ministries?

LOU ANN: Not to speak of.

GRACE (*to* MANICURIST NO. 2): That lady behind me should count her blessings. She's complaining that her church doesn't have any women's ministries. I wish that was my problem! My church has so many women's ministries, I don't get a moments rest!

LOU ANN (*to* MANICURIST NO. 1): Did you hear that lady behind me? She's talking about her church and all the women's ministries it has going.

GRACE (*to* MANICURIST NO. 2): But, what's really lacking at my church is a good youth program.

LOU ANN (*eavesdropping again, then comments to* MANICURIST NO. 1): Well, that is one thing I can say, our youth department is excellent. We've always had a good youth department.

GRACE (*to* MANICURIST NO. 2): Did you hear that? She's got a great youth program at her church! Our youth department's a disaster! Nothing's ever going on.

LOU ANN (*to* MANICURIST NO. 1): Our youth are always on the go!

GRACE (*to* MANICURIST NO. 2): I suppose her children's church program is fantastic, too.

LOU ANN (*to* MANICURIST NO. 1): Our children's church program is fantastic, too . . .

GRACE (*to* MANICURIST NO. 2): What did I tell you?

LOU ANN (*to* MANICURIST NO. 1): But our drama department could use a lot of help.

GRACE (*to* MANICURIST NO. 2): My church is just the opposite. Our drama department is great, but our children's church program is lacking.

LOU ANN (*to* MANICURIST NO. 1): And our services are too short.

GRACE (*to* MANICURIST NO. 2): Our services always run too long!

LOU ANN (*to* MANICURIST NO. 1): And we hardly ever have guest speakers or singing groups. It gets tiresome!

GRACE (*to* MANICURIST NO. 2): We're *always* having guest speakers and singing groups. It gets tiresome.

LOU ANN (*to* MANICURIST NO. 1): We never have any socials.

GRACE (*to* MANICURIST NO. 2): We have so many socials, I'm potlucked out!

LOU ANN (*to* MANICURIST NO. 1): That lady behind me doesn't know how good she's got it!

GRACE (*to* MANICURIST NO. 2): That lady behind me doesn't know how good she's got it!

LOU ANN (*to* MANICURIST NO. 1): I'd sure like to go to *her* church!

GRACE (*to* MANICURIST NO. 2): I'd sure like to go to *her* church!

LOU ANN (*looks at nails*): Oh, am I done?

MANICURIST NO. 1: That's it!

GRACE (*looks at nails*): I'm done?

MANICURIST NO. 2: All done!

(LOU ANN *and* GRACE *both tip the* MANICURISTS, *then stand up and turn around; when they see each other . . .*)

LOU ANN: Grace?

GRACE: Lou Ann?

MANICURIST NO. 1: Do you two know each other?

LOU ANN: Do we *know* each other?

GRACE: Of course, we know each other! We go to the same church!

(LOU ANN *and* GRACE *exit, talking excitedly to each other.*)

MANICURIST NO. 2 *(puzzled):* You mean, all this time they were both talking about the *same* church?!

MANICURIST NO. 1: Unbelievable, isn't it?

MANICURIST NO. 2: Well, I guess it's true what they say.

MANICURIST NO. 1: What's that?

MANICURIST NO. 2: The only "perfect" church is the one you don't attend!

USES, EXCUSES, EXCUSES

A Comedy Sketch

Characters:
DAN JACKSON
RICHARD BURNS, a television show host

Setting:
A door frame, or something to signify a front door

Props:
Hand-held microphone

▽

(Sketch opens with RICHARD BURNS knocking on the door. DAN JACKSON enters, sleepily. Dan is dressed in a bathrobe and slippers. His hair is standing straight up, he's unshaven, and has obviously just woken up. When he opens the door, he is greeted by a wide-awake, obnoxiously cheerful RICHARD BURNS, with microphone in hand.)

RICHARD: Good morning, sir!

DAN *(squinting from the bright sun, he yawns, then scratches his head)*: Is it morning already?

RICHARD *(laughs)*: It's been morning all morning, sir!

DAN *(groaning)*: Oh, no . . . you're not another one of those door-to-door comedians, are you?

RICHARD *(laughing)*: No, no, sir . . . I'm Richard Burns, host of the new television show called, "It's Sunday Morning . . . so Why Aren't You in Church?" Have you watched our show?

DAN *(trying to wake up)*: Uh, . . . no . . . I can't say I have. *(Bewildered)* What'd you say the name of it was again?

RICHARD: "It's Sunday Morning . . . so Why Aren't You in Church?"

DAN: Catchy title.

RICHARD: Well, what we do is go around from house to house every Sunday morning to find out why people, such as yourself, are not in church when they know they should be. So, tell me, Mr. . . . ?

DAN: Jackson. Uh, Dan Jackson.

RICHARD: Well, then, Mr. Dan Jackson . . . why don't you look right into the camera there and tell our television audience why you, sir, are not in church this morning. And you'd better make it good, Mr. Jackson, remember all America is watching!

DAN *(still quite bewildered, he looks at* RICHARD, *then looks toward imaginary camera, turns back to* RICHARD *again)*: Am I dreaming?

RICHARD *(laughs)*: A perfectly normal reaction, Mr. Jackson. Most folks are indeed surprised when we show up at their door and catch them staying home from church on Sunday morning.

DAN: I bet they are!

RICHARD: You see, sir, it's easy to give an excuse to your pastor, your Sunday School teacher, and even the choir director. But it's a different story when you have to give an excuse to *(makes sweeping motion with his hand)* . . . America! So, c'mon, tell us, Mr. Dan Jackson, tell your fellow churchgoing, God-fearing, Bible-believing Americans who, I might add, faithfully videotape our show every Sunday so they can watch it *after* they return home from church, tell all of them why it is you decided to stay home from church today?

DAN *(defensive)*: Hey, it's not like I miss church *every* Sunday, you know! You just happened to catch me on a day off!

RICHARD: Oh? Do you take days off from God, Mr. Jackson?

DAN: Uh . . . no, I didn't mean it that way. I just stayed home today . . . Just one, lousy, little Sunday.

RICHARD *(talking into imaginary camera)*: One, lousy, little Sunday? *(Looks back to Dan)* Is *that* what you said, Mr. Jackson?

DAN: You know what I meant. I just stayed home this ONE time . . . And anyway, I had a good reason!

RICHARD: We'll be the judge of that, Mr. Jackson. So, tell us, just what is this "good" reason, and remember . . . *(makes sweeping motion with hand again)* they're watching!

DAN: Uh, yeah . . . well, the reason I stayed home from church today was . . . *(thinks for a moment)* I didn't feel well?

RICHARD: Are you asking us or telling us?

DAN: I don't know. Do I look sick to you?

RICHARD: Well, yes, you have been looking a little pale ever since this interview began. But, I really don't think we can count that.

DAN: Well, would you excuse a death in the family?

RICHARD: It depends. Who died?

DAN: My goldfish.

RICHARD: Was he a blood relative?

DAN: No, just an in-law.

RICHARD: Doesn't count.

DAN: Well, how about if I told you I'm expecting out-of-town guests?

RICHARD: *Are* you expecting out-of-town guests?

DAN: No, but how about if I told you that?

RICHARD *(impatient)*: Mr. Jackson . . . we're going to have to break for a commercial soon. Don't you want to clear this up before we have to cut?

DAN: All right, I'll tell you the truth.

RICHARD: Our show is dedicated to airing the truth, Mr. Jackson.

DAN: OK, I stayed home so I could sleep in. *Are you happy now?* I've spilled my guts, confessed on nationwide television . . . now, will you leave me alone?

RICHARD: So, that's it, huh? You stayed home so you could sleep in?

DAN: That's right! I stayed home so I could sleep in.

RICHARD: And *did* you sleep in?

DAN: No! *You* woke me up!

RICHARD: Then, you stayed home for nothing, didn't you, Mr. Jackson?

DAN: I guess I never really thought of it that way.

RICHARD: You would have been much better off at church, wouldn't you? Go ahead, speak right into the mike.

DAN: Well, yes, I suppose, but . . .

RICHARD: You mean, there's *more?* You have *more* to confess?

DAN: I was just going to say that even if I had gotten up in time to go to church, I didn't have anything to wear.

RICHARD *(dramatic):* You didn't have anything to wear? Mr. Jackson, I can make an appeal right now on the air! Our friends in television land will be more than happy to open their hearts and . . .

DAN *(cuts in):* No, no! It's not that I don't have clothes. I *do* have clothes. I have plenty of clothes! It's just that I don't, well, you know, I don't have "church" clothes.

RICHARD: Mr. Jackson *(sighs),* do you know we recently took a poll of our viewers to find out what they considered to be the *stupidest* excuse of them all for nonchurch attendance, and do you know which one they selected?

DAN: No "church" clothes?

RICHARD: Bingo!

DAN: Well, where did "Staying home to mow the lawn" come in?

RICHARD: It tied for second with "Not wanting to miss a favorite television program."

DAN: You guys are ruthless.

RICHARD: No, just picky when it comes to excuses.

DAN: All right, what about "Too many hypocrites in church." Even you've got to admit that's a good excuse.

RICHARD: Good and stupid. It came in a solid third.

DAN: OK, what about "It's my only day off"? Where did that place?

RICHARD: Fourth.

DAN: Well, it sounds like your audience has already precondemned all the usual "staying home from church" excuses. So, really, nothing I could have said would have been good enough for them.

RICHARD: No, now that's not true. It's just that they've heard all of *your* excuses before, and quite frankly, they're getting tired of reruns! The bottom line is, Mr. Jackson, if you're going to stay home from church, you'd better have a very, *very* good reason! And for goodness sakes, next time try to be more original! *(Looks into imaginary camera)* And so this concludes another segment of our show. Tune in again next week when our cameras catch another unsuspecting church absentee. We'll be going on location to the river to film all those weekend campers . . . to see what their excuses are. Believe me, folks, it ought to be good. So, until then, remember . . . *it's Sunday morning* . . . and come to think of it, why aren't *(points toward the imaginary camera)* you in church?